Bates McKillian

Picking Puppies
Copyright © 2020 by Bates McKillian

All rights reserved. No part of this publication may be reproduced, distributed, or transmitted in any form or by any means, including photocopying, recording, or other electronic or mechanical methods, without the prior written permission of the author, except in the case of brief quotations embodied in critical reviews and certain other non-commercial uses permitted by copyright law.

Tellwell Talent
www.tellwell.ca

ISBN
978-0-2288-3178-5 (Hardcover)
978-0-2288-3177-8 (Paperback)
978-0-2288-4845-5 (eBook)

<u>Dedication:</u>

To the gifts that keep on giving.

"When are we going to pick out our graduation presents?" grumbled Kailley impatiently as she peered at her calendar. Kailley was wearing a short-sleeved lavender cotton top that was tucked into her navy blue shorts. Her dirty blond hair was worn half down with a French braid parting the middle.

"I don't know," replied Jane good-naturedly as she looked up from her laptop. Jane was two minutes older than Kailley and her hair and skin were also two shades darker than her sister's. Jane wore her hair half up, half down, and her blue eyes had a tendency to sparkle whenever she smiled, which was all the time. Jane was wearing navy blue shorts paired with a light blue cotton t-shirt. "Maybe we will go to the animal shelter this weekend."

Identical twins Kailley and Jane Brady had just graduated from college and were restlessly awaiting the arrival of the puppies their father had promised them for graduation presents.

Kailley and Jane's parents, Mr. and Mrs. Brady, had to work Monday through Friday. In order to accommodate Mr. and Mrs. Brady's schedules, the four agreed that they would go to the shelter on Saturday.

Saturday finally arrived, and Kailley and Jane crammed into the middle row of the family's trusty blue minivan at 9:00 a.m. sharp. Both young women wore flip flops, large black sunglasses, white pearl earrings, shorts, and pastel-colored cotton t-shirts.

"Jane and I are patiently waiting in the van!" broadcasted Kailley out the van window as her parents moseyed on over. The young women had been waiting in the van for at least fifteen minutes. "There aren't going to be any puppies left by the time we get there," whined Kailley, utterly exasperated.

Mrs. Brady had stopped to crouch down to prune some of her geraniums along the way to the van. Mrs. Brady had shoulder length blond hair and prescription eye glasses. This morning she was wearing an orange button down blouse with brown slacks. The look was completed with her purse casually draped over her left shoulder.

Meanwhile, Mr. Brady was busy balancing his sports bag which contained a generous supply of snacks for the hour-long road trip. Mr. Brady was ex-military, as could be detected from his impeccable posture. On this particular Saturday morning, he wore his summer church attire consisting of black trousers, boat shoes, and a blue polo shirt. Mr. Brady's personal supply of snacks consisted of apples, Ritz crackers, a plum or two, and some Tootsie Roll lollipops just in case he became sleepy on the journey home from the shelter.

Twenty minutes later, the four Bradys had finally situated themselves inside the van. Mr. Brady sat behind the wheel with Mrs. Brady beside him in the passenger's seat. After everyone had settled into their seats, they were off to the animal shelter.

On route to the shelter, Mrs. Brady took this opportunity to remind Kailley and Jane of a few household rules.

"Now Kailley and Jane," began Mrs. Brady while haphazardly flipping down the passenger seat's sun visor. She proceeded to slide open the compact mirror on the sun visor and adjust it until each daughter was fully visible in her mirror.

"A puppy is a lot of work," resumed Mrs. Brady as she tilted the mirror down a centimeter or two.

"Your father and I are NOT going to be caring for this puppy. As college graduates, this puppy is to be your responsibility. You are to train the puppy, feed the puppy, walk the puppy, and clean up after the puppy; is that understood?" asked Mrs. Brady, her bluish green eyes darting from one daughter to the other.

"Yes ma'am," responded Kailley in an exuberant Southern drawl as her twinkling blue eyes met her mom's exacting bluish green eyes in the mirror.

"And you, Jane?" Mrs. Brady's inquisitive bluish green eyes were now peering quizzically at Jane who at the moment was absent-mindedly scrolling through her phone.

"Understood!" replied Jane with some gusto as her smiling blue eyes locked with her mom's.

Jane was a bit preoccupied at the moment as she had yet to select a name for her puppy. She was therefore perusing the list of puppy names she had compiled and was busy testing the names out one by one.

"McSherry, come here, boy," called Jane.

"Jane!" admonished Mr. Brady, aghast, his blue eyes glancing in the rearview mirror at his daughter as if she had said something foul. "You cannot name your puppy after our friend's last name," reprimanded Mr. Brady.

"Fine," responded Jane with a wink at Kailley, as she deleted McSherry from her list.

Kailley, on the other hand, was sitting contentedly in her seat and staring out the window. Kailley had already chosen her puppy's name. She was determined to get a female puppy and name her "Elly" after her idol, Eleanor Roosevelt, and also the iconic New York character from the film *Eloise at the Plaza*.

As Kailley gazed out the window, she envisioned Jane and her training their puppies to be therapy dogs.

The young ladies had graduated from a small college outside of Boston that was rooted in public service.

Oftentimes when they were headed to class, Kailley and Jane would run into people from the town walking their dogs through the college's campus. Naturally, Kailley and Jane could not resist, and so they would stop and ask if they could pet the dogs. These dog owners would frequently inform Kailley and Jane that their dogs were rescues from a local animal shelter or that they were training their dogs to be therapy dogs.

Initially, Kailley and Jane had thought they would each get a purebred puppy from a breeder.

However, after some consideration, they decided that rescuing a puppy from a shelter would not only be less expensive, but they would also be helping a puppy in need.

Infused with their college's spirit, the young women had aspirations of one day taking their puppies to visit patients at their local hospital in the hopes that they could bring the patients some joy.

"And we do not have to get a puppy," interjected Mrs. Brady, thereby blatantly interrupting Kailley's goodwill reveries. "If you do not see a puppy that you want, that is fine; we do not need a dog."

"What?" objected Kailley, utterly confounded.

From the time Kailley and Jane were three years old, the Brady's home had always been brimming with animals, whether it be hamsters, rabbits, goldfish, a baby squirrel that needed some TLC, or sometimes even a bird or two that would unexpectedly shoot out of the Brady's living room fireplace covered in ash.

Moreover, during Kailley and Jane's freshman year of college, their childhood dog, Tipsy, who they had also rescued from an animal shelter, had passed away.

Whenever Kailley and Jane returned home for the summer or for the holidays, the Brady's home felt somehow incomplete without a dog.

Now that Kailley and Jane had finished college and they were moving back home, it felt only right for the Bradys to get another pet or two.

Observing that Mrs. Brady had some serious reservations about adopting one puppy, never mind two, neither Kailley nor Jane thought it necessary to mention to their mother that they were in fact rescuing two puppies.

"And what about jobs?" Mrs. Brady spoke up again, whipping down her sun visor and readjusting her mirror for full visuals of her daughters. "Are you two going to be able to adequately raise a puppy while applying for jobs?" grilled Mrs. Brady.

"Yes, Mom, we have talked about this," said Jane pleasantly. "Kailley and I will resume our summer jobs of working as camp counselors in the mornings. We will see the puppies…"

Kailley shot Jane an electrified look of alarm at Jane's use of the word "puppies."

"Puppy," amended Jane tactfully. "We will see the puppy when we come home for lunch, and then in the evenings we will waitress at the country club. Daddy is going to be at home working on the house this summer, so he can watch the PUPPY when we are at work," explained Jane, emphasizing the word puppy.

Mr. Brady was a teacher and school had just ended. Mr. Brady intended to paint the Brady's home during his summer vacation. As he was going to be home for the summer, Mr. Brady had happily offered to watch the puppies while his daughters were at work.

"And what about applying for full-time jobs?" quipped Mrs. Brady, knowing that this was a particularly sore topic for recent college graduates.

"We will work our summer jobs, care for the puppy, and apply to full-time jobs," answered Kailley with a smile.

In college, Kailley had majored in history and Jane had majored in sociology. Being as neither knew with certainty what kind of career paths they wanted to pursue, they had each decided they would take the summer one day at a time.

Mr. Brady had hardly braked in front of the animal shelter before Jane slid the back door of the van open. "This is fine; you can drop us off here," directed Jane, as she and Kailley hopped out.

"Thank you," called Kailley, as the two young women speed-walked towards the shelter.

The smell of animal dander floored their nostrils as they stepped inside the shelter, but to Kailley and Jane it smelled like paradise. The two took off in separate directions looking for their respective puppies.

The walls of the shelter were lined with crates towering six feet tall. Each crate contained one or two puppies. As it was still early in the morning, some of the puppies were soundly sleeping. Others were intently observing the people who had entered the shelter, while the remaining puppies had taken it upon themselves to give a hearty greeting to all the perspective dog owners.

Jane noticed that the workers were dressed in black trousers and heather-gray polo shirts with the shelter's name inscribed on the pocket. Jane listened as a couple asked one of the workers if they could hold a little white terrier puppy.

The worker subsequently unlocked the crate and handed the couple the little fuzzy white puppy. The worker then instructed the couple to carry the puppy over to the holding area located at the front of the room where there was a counter to place the pup on.

After parking the van, Mr. and Mrs. Brady entered the shelter a few minutes later.

Equipped with his checkbook, Mr. Brady was ready to finalize the adoptions. Meanwhile, Mrs. Brady was armed with a handful of tissues covering her nose.

"I don't know about this, Joe," gasped Mrs. Brady as she momentarily uncovered her nose in order to get a bit of air. Mrs. Brady instantly crinkled her nose in disgust as she was again waylaid by the deplorable stench of the animal shelter.

"Let's just look at the puppies Joanne," advised Mr. Brady, and he led his wife over to the wall of crates.

Before long, Mrs. Brady's nose had adapted to the smell of the shelter and she was continuously summoning Kailley and Jane to her side to gush over a puppy that she thought they should adopt.

It wasn't long before Jane was cradling a black hound mixed lab that Mrs. Brady had spotted.

The puppy was charcoal black, aside from some gray on her chest and the tips of her toes. She had floppy black ears, intelligent chestnut brown eyes that gazed up angelically at Jane, and just a stub of a tail.

Noticing that Jane was in the holding area with a puppy, Kailley wandered over to say hello.

"Kailley, I think I found her," announced Jane. "Isn't she a darling?"

"She is beautiful," agreed Kailley.

"I don't know what I am going to call her," confessed Jane.

Kailley gave the pup a quick introductory pat on the head and looked into her chestnut brown eyes knowingly. "Her name is Mitsey," declared Kailley.

"Mitsey," repeated Jane, trying it out for size.

"Are you a Mitsey?" asked Jane, looking fondly at the little puppy in her arms. The pup wagged her stubby tail, making Jane laugh.

Just as Kailley was starting to feel a little overwhelmed with the number of puppies to choose from, a puppy then stuck her paws out of the crate to swat at Kailley's hands. "Hello, who are you?" greeted Kailley. Kailley noted that the puppy was a border collie mixed golden retriever.

"Excuse me; may I hold this puppy?" inquired Kailley, pointing to the furry black dog with a wisp of white across her chest. She had dangly black ears, long black legs, an inordinately long tail, and soulful brown eyes.

"Why certainly," obliged one of the workers.

The worker accordingly unlatched the lock. As soon as the crate popped open, the puppy shrank to the back of the crate.

The worker had to reach deep within the crate to pull the puppy forward. The puppy in turn spread out her long legs and latched onto the walls of the crate for dear life with her paws.

Kailley stared wide-eyed at the puppy's display of behavior.

"Maybe this is not the puppy for me after all," thought Kailley as the worker struggled to get the puppy out of the crate.

With a firm tug, the worker managed to pry the puppy out of the crate.

"Here you go," said the worker as she passed the puppy to Kailley. The pup in turn wrapped her front legs around Kailley's neck and linked her back legs around Kailley's waist.

"It is like holding a child," commented Kailley as she took in her family's incredulous looks.

Curious, the Bradys had wandered over to see the puppy that Kailley had requested to hold. One of the shelter's workers offered to hold Mitsey while Jane went over to meet Kailley's puppy. Mr. Brady now had a pen in one hand, as he was preparing to write a check at any second now, and Mrs. Brady was repeatedly dabbing at her nose as if checking to make sure it was still there.

The pup clearly was a bit distressed and now had a giant snot bubble dangling from her nose. The bubble swung backward and forward, threatening to burst at any moment.

"Would you look at that?" grinned Jane, marveling at the size of the bubble.

"At what?" asked Kailley, oblivious to the bubble. She craned her neck to get a good look at the puppy's face.

"It's going to pop!" shrieked Mrs. Brady as Kailley's neck made contact with the snot bubble.

With that, a glob of lukewarm goo slid down Kailley's neck.

"Yuck," declared Jane, slightly bemused.

"Aww, Kailley, you should put that one back. She is obviously sick, and she is very shy," pointed out Mrs. Brady.

"She is fine; she just has a cold," dismissed Kailley, undeterred as she carried the puppy over to the countertop in the holding area that ran around the perimeter of the front of the room. Kailley gently placed the puppy on the counter. The puppy wedged herself into the corner of the countertop until she was as far away as possible from Kailley.

Mr. Brady brought Kailley a paper towel to wipe the guck off.

Kailley thanked her father for the paper towel and dabbed at the puppy mucus on her neck.

Determined to win the despondent puppy over, Kailley stuck out her hand to let the puppy sniff her, but the puppy ignored her hand.

She tried to pet the puppy, but the puppy dodged her hand.

Kailley tried talking quietly to the puppy, but the puppy continued to cower in the corner.

Kailley refused to give up on the puppy.

Deciding to change tactics, Kailley then crumpled the mucky paper towel into a ball. She passed the paper towel ball across the counter from one hand to the other.

The puppy's chestnut brown eyes were now mesmerized by the ball and attentively followed the ball from one hand to the other. Without warning, the puppy suddenly pounced on the paper towel ball with her two front paws.

"Oh, so you do have game," challenged Kailley, smiling as the puppy backed up and stood on her toes, ready to squash the paper towel ball again. The puppy and Kailley continued to play with the paper towel.

"I am going to call you Elly," confided Kailley to the little black puppy. With that, the little puppy nudged Kailley's hand with her head, inviting a pat.

"Wow, look at her now!" remarked Jane, seeing the transformation in the puppy.

"Persistence and patience," responded Kailley with a relieved smile.

"Do you bark, Elly?" asked Kailley. Kailley imitated barking, but the puppy refused to make a sound. The other puppies in the shelter were now all barking including Mitsey who was showing off her trademark hound howl. "Ruff, ruff," imitated Kailley. "Maybe you are one of those dogs that do not bark," reasoned Kailley, and with that, Elly gave a tentative woof.

"I'll take this one," laughed Kailley. "Very nice, Elly," congratulated Kailley upon hearing Elly's bark.

"Oh no, Kailley; we are only getting one puppy," corrected Mrs. Brady, as she admired the docile hound in Jane's arms.

"Daddy said we could get two," retorted Kailley.

"He said what!" exclaimed Mrs. Brady, absolutely appalled. Mrs. Brady's eyes scanned the room with laser-like focus until she zeroed in on her husband who was talking quietly to an older dog. "JOE!!!" bellowed Mrs. Brady. The puppies in the shelter all stopped barking as everyone in the shelter turned to stare at Mrs. Brady.

Mrs. Brady was now biting her tongue, which signaled to Kailley and Jane that their mother was very mad. Kailley and Jane took this as their cue to make themselves scarce and hurried over to far side of the shelter.

After a lengthy conversation between Mr. and Mrs. Brady, with Mr. Brady looking appropriately abashed for having promised each daughter a puppy for graduation without Mrs. Brady's approval, the Bradys at last signed the adoption papers and agreed to pick up the puppies later that day, as the shelter first had to process their paperwork.

Kailley and Jane were scheduled to waitress at the country club that evening, and so Mr. and Mrs. Brady volunteered to pick up the puppies.

Later that night, dressed in their waitressing apparel of black ties, white button-down shirts, black aprons, black pants, and of course black sneakers, Kailley and Jane turned the key and opened the front door of their home to the welcome sight of two little black puppies slipping and sliding across the hardwood floors to greet them.

Mr. and Mrs. Brady had been tending to the puppies while Kailley and Jane were waitressing. Mr. and Mrs. Brady smiled happily at one another as Kailley and Jane sat on the floor to play with their puppies.

Finally, the Bradys' home felt complete.

The End.

www.ingramcontent.com/pod-product-compliance
Lightning Source LLC
LaVergne TN
LVHW072016060526
838200LV00059B/4684